D0431948

Christine Mather's

SANTA FE
CHRISTMAS

To: *Amanda and Thais*

From: *Mom, with love*

Christine Mather's
SANTA FE
CHRISTMAS

CLARKSON POTTER/PUBLISHERS
NEW YORK

Copyright ©1993 by Christine Mather
Illustrations copyright © 1993 by the Estate of Willard Clark

All rights reserved. No part of this book may be reproduced or transmitted in any form or by any means; electronic or mechanical, including photocopying, recording, or by any information storage and retrieval system, without permission in writing from the publisher.

Published by Clarkson Potter/Publishers, 201 East 50th Street, New York, New York 10022. Member of the Crown Publishing Group.

Random House, Inc. New York, Toronto, London, Sydney, Auckland.

CLARKSON N. POTTER, POTTER and colophon are trademarks of Clarkson N. Potter, Inc.

Manufactured in Japan

Designed by Altemus Creative Servicenter

Library of Congress Cataloging-in-Publication Data

Mather, Christine.
     Santa Fe Christmas / Christine Mather.—1st ed.
        p.   cm.
     Includes index.
     1. Christmas—New Mexico—Santa Fe. 2.
Christmas decorations—New Mexico—Santa Fe. 3. Cookery, America—Southwestern style. 4. Santa Fe (N.M.)—Social life and customs. I. Title.
GT4986.N6M38   1993   93-2736
394.2'68282'0978956—dc20   CIP

ISBN 0-517-59246-0

10 9 8 7 6 5 4 3 2 1

First Edition

Photography Credits

Numbers indicate pages. Numbers in parentheses indicate archive negative numbers.

Code: T-Top; TR-Top Right; TL-Top Left; C-Center; CL-Center Left; R-Right; L-Left; B-Bottom; BR-Bottom Right; BL-Bottom Left.

Eduardo Fuss: 22, 24 CL, 26, 29, 31 T & B, 32, 33, 42, 49 T, 51, 62 L, TR, & BR, 65 R, 67, 87
Terry Husebye: 78
Vicente Martinez: 26 L, 27 T & B, 35, 88 T
Christine Mather: 36 T, 38, 39, 40 B, 41, 58 C, 59, 61 T, 63, 72 C, 79 T & B, 84, 86 L
Museum of New Mexico, Photo Archives: 11 (36461); 15 (91132); Dana B. Chase 12 (134176); Aaron B. Craycroft 10 (13695); Jesse L. Nusbaum 9 (61456), 14 (61440); T. Harmon Parkhurst 13 (47295), 16 (3560)
Mark Nohl, Courtesy of *New Mexico Magazine*: 7, 22, 28, 30, 34, 45, 47, 48, 49 B, 50 T, 61 B, 64
Jack Parsons: 23, 24 TL, 25 BL, 27 C, 36 B, 37, 40 T, 46, 49 C, 50 B, 56 L, 58 T & B, 60, 65 L, 66 L & R, 70, 72 T & B, 73, 74, 75, 76, 77, 80, 81, 82, 83, 86 R, 88 B, 89
Gene Peach: 19, 24, 25, 52, 53 T & B, 54, 56 R, 57, 69
Bransom Reynolds: 21 T & B
Illustration Credits: All illustrations are by Willard Clark with the help of Kevin Ryan. Copyrighted by the Estate of Willard Clark.

Acknowledgments

Like the gifts of children, Santa Fe's gifts come in small ways throughout the year and are often intangible—fleeting memories of smells, sights, and gatherings. All of the illustrations here, whether photograph or drawing, capture this fleeting world of emotion and nature. My warm thanks to all who contributed their art to this book. Willard Clark's illustrations capture the soul of the little town. I am grateful that Willard agreed to work on this project with the help of his grandson Kevin Ryan and his mother Doris Clark Senutovitch who embraced the inclusion of Willard's work in this publication. For the photographs I thank the Photo Archives of the Museum of New Mexico, Jack Parsons, Eduardo Fuss, Mark Nohl, Gene Peach, Vicente Martinez, Terry Husebye, and Bransom Reynolds. Those who opened their hearts and homes, and gave of themselves include Susan Topp Weber, Forrest Moses, Nedra Matteucci, the folks at the Wheelwright Museum, Lynette Wagner, Cordelia Thomas Snow, Reynalda Dinkel, Anita Thomas, and Josie Gallegos. My special thanks to chef Paul Hunsicker, of Paul's Restaurant, for his recipes and advice. At Clarkson Potter, season's greetings to one and all but especially to my friend Lauren Shakely, and to Howard Klein, Kristin Frederickson, Renato Stanisic, Joan Denman, Laurie Stark, and Amy Boorstein. Greetings and thanks are due to my agent Deborah Geltman and designer Robert Altemus.

For my family, who give of themselves all year round, my love.

CONTENTS

Introduction

A Christmas story is a gift from the teller to those he loves. Most often it is a gift to children—for, in the end, Christmas remains the property of children. The story of Christmas is a story of one special Child and a poignant reminder that within each

newborn lies the same potential for salvation. Christmas also carries an elaborate myth of the purity and innocence of childhood that we all hope to regain through our memories of childhood or through joyful observation of our own children. The ingenuousness of childhood, with its willing belief in the miraculous delivery of gifts from the unseen, may have now become a marketing tool for a consumer society, but not so very long ago, in all American communities, the celebration of the Nativity of Christ was above all a solemn religious holiday.

Until just a few years ago, Santa Fe was a poor community with little access to manufactured goods. The tale of life was most frequently a recounting of difficult realities—how much food was in storage, how difficult the journey was, how many oxen the priest owed the carpenter, how cold it was that day. The less stolid aspects of life—the music and poetry, storytelling and imaginings—for the most part went unrecorded and were passed on orally, in the time-honored traditions of repetition and reenactment. So it was too with the activities of the Christmas season. Santa Feans lived outside the emphasis upon lavish feasts, glamorous decorations, Christmas trees, Santa Clauses, gift giving, and many other rites of our contemporary American Christmas. Instead, all of the celebratory traditions were simple and charming annual rites that emphasized a coming together, a generous heart, a playful humor, and a deep faith.

The real gift of Christmas has, after all, very little to do with store sales, parades, figgy pudding, reindeer, or wish lists. The vanity and excess of a material celebration are not often held up to the scrutiny which Dickens so unerringly brought to bear in his morality tale *A Christmas Carol*. It isn't good business. Yet

Opposite: A lone figure on Santa Fe's Plaza on a dark winter's day, as captured by photographer Jesse L. Nusbaum, ca. 1912.

the business of Christmas is not one of riches. When we search back through the gifts we have given and received, the gifts we value most are those from the heart—the lump of clay lovingly

fashioned into a precious paperweight or the mayonnaise jar transformed with paper and paint into the pencil holder that sits for years on the desk, long after the expensive sweater lies forgotten in the drawer.

Santa Fe at Christmas offers this same gift from the heart—a gift of crisp, clean air filled with the sharp scent of burning pinyon, of bonfires that light the way to Christmas, a gift of simplicity, of humor, and of love. The offerings are personal and tinged with the slight sadness of the passing of time, but are also imbued with the deep joy of being alive in the heightened awareness of a powerful physical world.

The Hispanic community of Santa Fe traditionally celebrated the Christmas season throughout the month of December and well into January. Although the northern European emphasis upon Saint Nicholas was absent, the holiday in New Mexico shared many aspects with the Christian celebration. But it was the delightful local traditions that came to dominate the way Christmas was celebrated in the region. It was a true season, beginning around the feast of the Virgin of Guadalupe on December 12 and concluding with Epiphany on January 6. Records of the colonial period give the barest acknowledg-

An early photograph of New Mexico's Christmas play Los Pastores, left, shows the archival angels of Heaven and Hell about to begin battle.

11

ment of the events of Navidad, but the recollections of older inhabitants suggest a season greatly anticipated by young and old, full of celebration and wonderful food.

The energy and enthusiasm for the Holy Days of Christmas was not limited to the His-

Matachines dancers pose with a young Malinche, far right. Performed in both Native and Hispanic villages at Christmas, the dance reflects the Spanish conquest.

panic community but found a reflection in the rituals of the Native Americans, who celebrated with

traditional activities that marked the change of seasons as well as through Catholic ceremonies, often held in conjunction with the traditional rituals. This merging of different rituals and beliefs, never an exact or complete union, gave to the entire region a season of celebration which was unique and continues to be so today.

The final ingredient to this mix of ritual, event, and belief came in the mid-nineteenth century with the arrival of the Anglo-Americans. Despite their own initial reactions to the people of the area—ranging from bafflement to horror—in time, the Anglo-American community both joined and added to the traditional celebrations. Of course, not all of this merging of traditions was harmonious, nor was it done without the loss of some native traditions, but what remains is a distinctly Santa Fe way of celebration.

Within the story of Santa Fe Christmas lies the deeper story of life on the frontier, the rush of events that followed the big wars, and the struggle between very different cultures, for perhaps no other American community lives so closely with the rough edges of diverse peoples coming together. Within Santa Fe's day-to-day existence lies the unusual awareness of the first people to inhabit the lands of North America, Native Americans; the second people who came to conquer and settle, Hispanic Americans; and the third people, a seemingly relentless amalgam of drives and ambitions, the Anglo-Americans. This is not just our history but our present, which, when forgotten, leads to conflict and loss. The ability to come together, to hold together as family and friends, and to relish our diversity, is a significant achievement and seems most poignant at Christmas. It is this shared experience, so in keeping with the sentiment of the season that is the subject of this book.

When the snow falls seriously and steadily in Santa Fe, heralding the arrival of the Christmas season, the town reverts to its former self and becomes again a place of narrow, empty streets with low-slung tan buildings and walls directly abutting the streets. The plaza, the center of town from which all activity and sentiment spread, is the staging area for one Christmas celebration after another. Ancient plays reenacting the life of

Christ, bonfires and multiple homemade lights, Santa Claus and hundreds of Christmas shoppers staring intently at the Native American crafts for sale—all bring life to the center of the town, stealing the thunder of the shopping malls that

Baking bread in a horno at Cochiti Pueblo, ca. 1920. Luckily, the oven could accommodate the large volume of holiday baking.

have disintegrated the old squares of most small American towns. The shoppers walk in snow. They brave the cold, armed with hot cider and cookies—not just any cookies, but *bizcochitos*

A large harvest of pinyon nuts, **left**, *was a welcome cash crop for Santa Feans.* **Above:** *A major ice-gathering effort near Las Vegas, New Mexico.*

(the state cookie), fortification for those seekers of the perfect gift. The gifts they seek—handmade, small, and simple—transcend uniformity. Picked out one by one, they are carried home as tokens of the uniqueness of the receiver and the love the giver holds for them.

No wonder the town fills up at Christmas—the hotels jammed, the sidewalks busy, the warm cider or chocolate flowing, the old traditions of the region well attended—Santa Fe at Christmas is a place not for the observer but for the participant. Everyone burns pinyon pine, known for its distinctive odor, sweet and crisp in the cold, thin air; even on the chilliest nights, Santa Feans go out into the night to smell it. Like the smell, the taste of Christmas in Santa Fe is sharp; the food is fit for a peasant and is the stuff of the New World—corn, beans, squash, chile, chocolate. At dusk, the foothills, once white and dotted with pinyon pine, turn pink with dramatic shadows. The light of evening transforms the natural world and makes its true mystery visible.

It is possible to go back in time: Turn out the lights, leave the car in the driveway, have a bowl of *posole*, take a deep breath of pinyon-scented air, and step into Santa Fe at Christmas. ✱

CUSTOMS OF THE COUNTRY

Winter Comes

Life at 7,000 feet means snow. Santa Fe snow has all of the variations that might be expected at this altitude—from dry, thin, and swirling to thick, wet, and sticky. Snow can quickly turn to sequins reflecting back every light, glittering in the dry air of day

or night. Trapped in the pinyon pine needles, clinging to the leafless aspen, or plastered against the adobe walls, snow has the most astounding ability to transform the world completely in a matter of hours.

Santa Feans seem to have a remarkable ability to ignore many of the effects of snow. Unlike the resigned inhabitants of the East and Midwest, we choose not to shovel unless absolutely necessary and then only a narrow path on a sidewalk. Sooner or later the sun will do the job. This is the land of *poco tiempo*, which, loosely translated, means that eventually it will get done and in the meantime, there is no need to worry. As far as roads are concerned, it does mean that New Mexico has a tendency to shut down major highways and that folks are forever being trapped in Moriarty or Gallup until the sun comes out.

This year, winter came early, so that the jack-o'-lantern froze solid to the porch before we had a chance to light the match. Halloween night brought dancing fairy princesses racing from the school gym to the car in a run of secondhand-

store taffeta and satin high heels. No trick-or-treating this year—it was far too cold. The early freezing weather and heavy snows brought to a quick end the equally rushed activity of the pinyon pickers. Pinyon nuts once fueled families through the long winter months, from the time of the Native Americans into the twentieth century, but it had been many, many years since the pinyon harvest in the foothills around Santa Fe had been so abundant. Cars lined the Old Las Vegas Highway and many elderly picnickers set off with their empty lard cans to participate in the harvest. By Christmas, winter had dazzled us with snow in the mountains and many nights of stars behind the rising smoke of the pinyon log fires. ✶

Preceding page: *Snowbird dance at San Ildefonso Pueblo, 1935. Opposite: Snow on Upper Canyon Road covers a little courtyard seen through an adobe arch.*

The Badlands are
transformed into a
fairyland with the
winter snows, far left.
Above: A snow goose
in flight. A mule deer
on a wintry day in
the San Juan Moun-
tains, left.

Snow, the great level-
er, blankets the calm
of an Indian woman
by sculptor Doug
Hyde, above, *and fills*
the empty spaces of a
tiled parapet, right.

Snow highlights some
of Santa Fe's native
forms, including the
Fine Arts Museum,
above left, ristras,
center left, *and adobe
walls*, left.

Guadalupe

Before Christmas could arrive in the New World, Christianity had to make its entrance. Although the missionary zeal of the Spaniards was unsurpassed, native populations were not successfully converted to Christianity until sometime in the sixteenth century, when the Virgin of Guadalupe miraculously appeared to an impoverished Indian, Juan Diego, outside of Mexico City. As the Virgin explained to Juan Diego, she appeared to him alone so that the most humble would be accepted by the most powerful. The miracle of the Virgin of Guadalupe, which is today observed on December 12 by Native Americans and Hispanics alike, became one of the first of many Christian celebrations in the New World. ✶

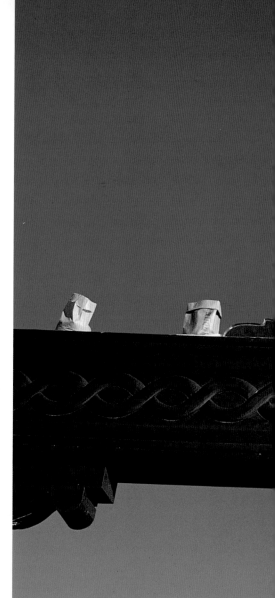

Special celebrations for the Virgin of *Guadalupe, far left,* are held in churches throughout the region. At twilight, parishioners in Taos celebrate with a solemn procession of the Virgin through the snow-packed streets, bottom right.

Las Posadas

The search made by Mary and Joseph for a place in which she might give birth is a tale reenacted each year in Santa Fe and the Hispanic villages in the mountains. In the early reenactment, a village couple traveled to nine different homes on nine consecutive nights (a novena), as if searching for a *posada* (inn)—thus the name of the plays, Las Posadas. All of those who had followed the couple on the journey through the cold and snowy neighborhood converged on the last home, where the couple would at last be welcomed.

Today in Santa Fe, the plaza serves as a stage for the drama, which is performed on a single night. Afterward, hundreds of onlookers enter the courtyard of the Palace of the Governors for hot chocolate and *bizcochitos*. ✶

The forces of good and evil contrast with one another in a local play, left. Good will eventually triumph and all will go forward to worship the Christ Child. Above: A young Mary.

*The Shepherds at
Las Golindrinas*, left.
*A performance in the
church at Las Tram-
pas*, above. *Mary on
a burro goes in
search of shelter in a
reenactment of Las
Posadas*, right.

A pensive Wise Man at an annual performance of Los Pastores, left. A happy devil, opposite, expresses an obvious delight in playing one of the most popular antagonists of the season.

Los Pastores

Of all the festivities of the Christmas season, none were so greatly relished as the performances of the shepherds' story—Los Pastores. In the New World, native populations and local colonists were treated to plays of Adam and Eve, the appearances of the Virgin of Guadalupe, the Shepherds, and the Three Wise Men. Performed by parish members, acting groups, or families, these church-sponsored events were enormously popular. But the story of the shepherds remained the favorite, inspiring numerous scripts passed from generation to generation, either orally or in simple *cuadernos* (notebooks). In New Mexico, not only were scripts passed down, but individual roles as well, from father to son. The success of Los Pastores was due in large measure to the often off-color nature of the characters and their lines, as over the years the story strayed from its purely churchly moorings into the realm of farce. The buffoon roles and that of Lucifer were especially coveted. These characters, who babbled on in long, hilarious soliloquies, embodied the spirit of Los Pastores—the only mystery play to promote carryings-on of a nonreligious nature. ✲

The scene of Mary and Joseph in the manger, opposite, or traveling to Bethlehem is reenacted annually. Right: A scene carved in wood of the Holy Couple on their journey to Bethlehem.

Away in a Manger

A more respectful but equally popular form of re-creation than the Pastores farces is the Nativity scene. Life-size Nativities with life-size figures or even live participants can still be found in many parts of New Mexico during the season. Perched on hillsides around New Mexico or prominently displayed upon the parapet of La Fonda, the inn at the end of the Santa Fe Trail, Nativity scenes flourish in a town named for the saint who brought this custom to the world—La Villa Real de Santa Fe de San Francisco. ✻

The pueblos are alive throughout the Christmas season with celebrations of dance and song. A wintry day at Taos Pueblo, opposite. Drummers and dancers at Pojoaque Pueblo, right. A dancer at San Ildefonso Pueblo, below.

The Pueblos

Along the waterways of northern New Mexico, and down through the Rio Grande Valley, live the Pueblo Indians. They live upon the lands of their ancestors, and their history is far, far older than any other history of this land. In many ways their culture has nothing to do with the world of Christmas and European sentiment. Their languages, their settlements, their beliefs, all predate the Christian influence and are rooted in the rhythmic cycle of life in which man plays but a small role. Following the period of grace and gratitude for the harvests of summer's bounty, the world moves into its winter cycle and the Pueblo moves

36

with it. It is a time when natural life has moved underground, has died away; when darkness comes sooner and stays longer; when nothing grows. The prayer for the return of life is as old as man. Among the Pueblos, a part of this prayer comes in the form of dance and music.

Native American dance and music are two of the most enriching elements of life in New Mexico. Although Santa Feans have the opportunity to witness this conjunction of movement, music, spirituality, and nature all year round, the Pueblo dances of Christmas Eve and Christmas have special meaning. They are not performances, but an affirmation of all that it means to be alive.

When the drums begin in the cold of a winter morning on the plazas of the pueblos, the dancers are surrounded by people from many different cultures, not just the dancers' own. They come no longer out of a sense of curiosity but out of a need to participate in a ritual that has no words, a ritual that is timeless and soothing and connected to an unseen force larger than themselves. ✯

Drummers and singers, above, set a steady rhythm for dancers like the Deer dancer, right, who mimics his namesake's graceful movements throughout the dance.

38

The most intact of the pueblos, the Pueblo of Taos north of Santa Fe, left, echoes the shape of the mountains behind it. Oblivious to the mud, the dance continues, below left. The warmth of a Pendleton blanket protects the shoulders of a Pueblo man during a dance, opposite.

O LITTLE TOWN

Lighting the Way

A part of the ritual of return and renewal in Santa Fe is a celebration of light. Lights are placed along the streets to lead the way to Christmas, to call and recall, to beckon forth the Christ Child, the Santo Niño, into the world and guide Him to the bonfires of the faithful. Square stacks of pinyon pine *(luminarias)* lead to the portals of the church where bigger bonfires call the worshipper to Him. Between the bonfires, simple votive candles are placed in paper bags and secured with a few handfuls of sand. These small lanterns, whose tan color blends with the surrounding adobe, line the walls and streets, decorate walkways, churches, homes, and even trees, and beckon all to join in the celebration of the night in which the world was transformed and illuminated.

Santa Feans are extremely sensitive about what constitutes a *luminaria* as opposed to a *farolito*, a touchy distinction that leaves the rest of the country baffled. Patiently and ritu-

Preceding page: Pigeons on the Plaza in Santa Fe. The Inn of Loretto stands as a massive monument to the farolito, or in this case the "electrolito," throughout the Christmas season.

alistically, the local papers spell out the fine points for the uninitiated every year. A letter to the editor appearing a few years back sets the record straight and updates the language to reflect changing times:

Since 'tis the season to be jolly, I thought it time to set the record straight for newcomers about some of our more quaint customs in Santa Fe.
1. *Luminarias:* small bonfires usually found at the entrance to house, along streets and the like; not recommended for rooftops as one of our newspapers suggested recently.
2. *Farolitos:* small paper bags partially filled with sand and containing a slow burning candle, not to be confused with:
3. *Electrolitos:* electrified plastic bags placed upon the firewalls of all Downtown businesses in place of *farolitos*.
4. *Ristralitos:* electrified *ristras*, real or plastic.

While the latter two customs are found with increasing frequency around town, they should not be confused with "true" Santa Fe style; they are in fact kitsch, and on a par with bandana-clad, howling coyotes, whatever the size.

Cordelia Thomas Snow
Santa Fe
Albuquerque Journal North, December 15, 1990

As Christmas Eve approaches, many local groups begin organizing for the setting out of the lights. Entire neighborhoods join in an effort to place the *farolitos* along the homes' walls and

Farolitos *everywhere,* **in *treetops,* above,** **and on the *windowsill*** **of a *little adobe house,*** **opposite.**

roads. At dusk, the cars are banished and the entire city can walk the old streets, admiring the enchanted scene set by the humble *farolitos*. It is a scene of indescribable charm and beauty—the snow has on the hues of the evening light, the streets are low and quiet, the little lights reveal the contours of the small homes and narrow streets— as the people talk quietly in greeting. "Above thy deep and dreamless sleep the silent stars go by." ✫

Preceding pages: *A compound at twilight reflects the beauty of a simple custom,* right. *Fancy paper-bag farolitos, top. A youngster helps out,* center. *A lovely farolito cross made for Christmas Eve,* bottom.

Farolitos *above gates,* above. *A small home,* right, *combines Christmas lights and farolitos.*

Luminarias *and*
farolitos, opposite and
above, *call to the*
faithful and provide
warmth for singers,
worshippers, and on-
lookers alike, who fill
the streets on Christ-
mas Eve. Preparing
the **luminaria, left.**

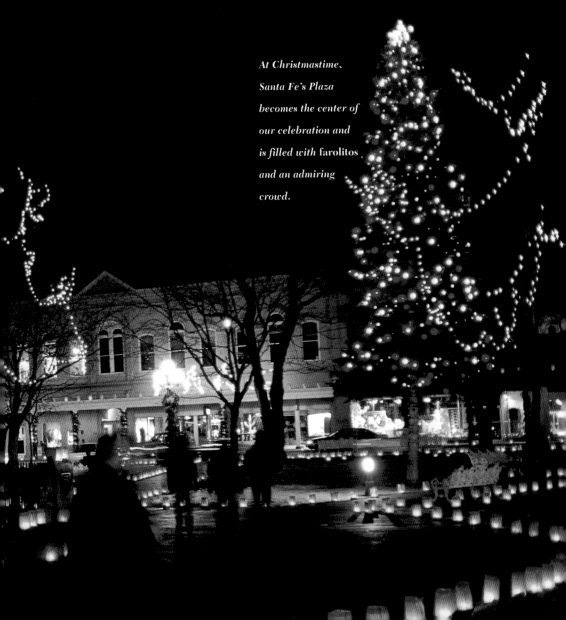

*At Christmastime,
Santa Fe's Plaza
becomes the center of
our celebration and
is filled with farolitos
and an admiring
crowd.*

A shopper passes the decorated turquoise posts of Sena Plaza, right, while the Fenn Gallery, far right, prepares for the season with an array of farolitos.

Above: *A zany chair in Madrid, an abandoned mining town near Santa Fe, is part of this tiny community's all-out Christmas celebration.*

All Through the Streets

Santa Fe prepares itself for Christmas by using the simplest of materials, pine boughs cut from the ever-present pinyons and ponderosa pines, *farolitos*, a red ribbon or two for contrast, and perhaps a string or two of plain white lights. Somehow these simple objects make a far greater statement than the giant plastic angels and Santa Clauses that grace many other American cities. Perhaps it is because the wreaths hang on well-worn and weathered gates, the *farolitos* line ancient adobe homes, the little white lights dance in the barren branches of the trees, and the pine boughs are wound around the posts of the portals. Each year the town returns to the same modest manner of celebration. ✶

For decades, the town of Madrid has put special effort into its decorations, including not only the town's buildings but those of the surrounding hillsides as well.

This page: All the wonderful weathered gates of Santa Fe are used as backdrops for handmade wreaths and decorations.

Snow clings to a
coyote fence,
opposite. *A flourish
of poinsettias,* left,
*known locally
as Flor de Noche
Buena. A yucca,*
below, *covered in
snow.*

Nature Decorates

Pinyon trees with puffs of snow, *canales* (drain spouts that allow the water to fall off the flat roofs of Santa Fe's houses) dripping with sheets of icicles, blue-gold skies at evening, and pink fairy snow on the foothills accented by deep green dots of juniper and pine, a million crystal ice patterns, and more—man composes beauty, but nature tosses forth these scenes of intense beauty. Snow sits upon the mountains, not just a blanket but a giant river that will fill the *acequias* (aqueductlike ditches used to deliver water to the fields) and flow into the gardens all summer long. Once frozen solid during the Little Ice Age, the Rio Grande flows on in every season, but the Santa Fe River slows to a halt, released slightly by the strong midday sun only to refreeze in the evening

cold. By Christmas the Sangre de Cristo Mountains are fully blanketed by snow, forming the backdrop for the city in winter. ✶

Wreaths and Ristras

Each fall brings to Santa Fe the raw material for the town's most favored flavor. Across New Mexico, Anaheim and Hatch chiles are harvested just at the moment they begin to turn from green to the bright red of a fully ripe chile. They are then tied to each other to form long, heavy strings called *ristras*. In the fall, thousands of *ristras* hang from fruit and vegetable stands and from the walls of homes. Once the chiles are dry, they are used to make the hot spicy dish of the same name, which is virtually New Mexico's recipe.

As elsewhere in the country, evergreen wreaths adorn doorways and walls throughout Santa Fe, but the red chile wreath (a *ristra* with its ends connected to form a circle) is the town's holiday trademark. ✷

Santa Feans prefer wreaths made from chiles strung to dry. **Above:** *A young woman prepares the chiles for a* ristra.

Bay leaves and cinna-mon sticks become an aromatic decoration, opposite. At Susan's Christmas Shop, above, a wreath of little Pueblo bells beckons. Aged doors and a pair of wreaths at Santa Fe East Gallery, right.

A charming water-color, ca. 1930s, depicts a koshare, *a Pueblo clown, offering a chicken to Santa Claus. Santa heads south, below, and appears at the dances on Christmas Day at San Ildefonso Pueblo in shocking contrast to the dancers,* **right.**

Santa Fe Santas

There have always been many *santos* and *santas* (male and female saints) in Santa Fe, but the Santa best known by the rest of the country, the red-capped, jolly fellow that fell down the chimneys elsewhere, never set foot in the town of Santa Fe until well into the nineteenth century, when local Hispanics began to marry newly arrived Eastern Americans. While the Roman Catholic, Spanish-speaking New Mexicans accepted this odd, jolly new saint into the local pantheon, Native Americans viewed him with suspicion: Who was this white-faced fellow with a bag of things? Even today, Santa Fe Santas are a bit offbeat. ✫

HOME FOR CHRISTMAS

As it is around the world, the heart of Christmas in Santa Fe is at home. Santa Fe is a close-knit town of extended families, some of which can trace their heritage back to the first colonists. In the New Mexico territory, exchanging gifts was not common

at the holidays until well into the nine-teenth century, and Christmas trees were a rarity into the twentieth, but simple decorations were always a part of the annual festivities. The first decorations were part of the preparation of the church for the Holy Day. Specially carved Nativities, costly candles, and modest strings of paper flowers were prepared. In native churches, pine boughs were the main ornamental element.

Preceding page: Santa Fe ornaments fill a tree. Opposite: Our house at Christmas. Ornaments include gourds carved with petroglyph designs, miniature kachinas, and blown eggs painted to resemble Pueblo pottery.

At home, the most elaborate preparations were performed in the kitchen. Young children, especially those from the poorest of village families, traveled from house to house, asking for edible hand-outs with a sweet cry of "Miss Christmas!" There were bogey-men to scare the youngsters, but like the "Miss Christmas" tradition, this practice gradually faded out, replaced by new ways of celebrating that arrived with the Anglo-American immigrants. The first Christmas trees and store-bought ornaments appeared relatively recently in Santa Fe's history. Besides lifelike, life-size, and living Nativities, most New Mexicans cherish a person-al *nacimiento,* which they add to each year. It is opened first among the decorations, and packed regretfully at the end of the season. In Mexico City, immense markets of plaster Nativity figures continue, to this day, to supply the undiminished need to keep the crèche growing, one that results in a combination of Noah's Ark, Eden, and Beth-lehem. Native Americans led their own ritual of bringing little clay animals to the church on Christmas Eve so that they could be blessed. Ul-timately, all of these small figures turned up as a wonderful and bewildering array of folk Christ-mas tree ornaments, made by Native, Hispanic, and Anglo artisans alike.

71

New Mexicans search the Indian Market in August for the beasts of December, gathering bear fetishes from the Zuni Pueblo and turtles from Santa Clara Pueblo, owls from Acoma Pueblo and storytellers from Cochiti. A September trip to Cordova might yield Lopez carvings of quail or the Holy Child in cedar. Little deer dancers come from San Juan Pueblo, angels from Jemez, mud toy sheep from Navajo country, and tin ornaments from the Spanish Market. Children at school fashion "god's eyes" while a neighbor might contribute tiny red velveteen chiles—all for a true Santa Fe Christmas tree. The city's rich and eclectic heritage is never more prominent than in its homes at Christmastime. ✶

In keeping with the ways of the West: lights shaped like cowboy boots, a candy cane snake by Paul Lutonsky, and a simple kachina ornament. **Far right:** *A gourd painted with petroglyph-like Indian figures.*

A shooting star, above, is a wonderful example of Plains Indian beadwork. Santa Fe decorates with an adobe home candle, above right, or a basketful of Navajo dolls, right. Opposite: A Christmas angel from Venezuela.

74

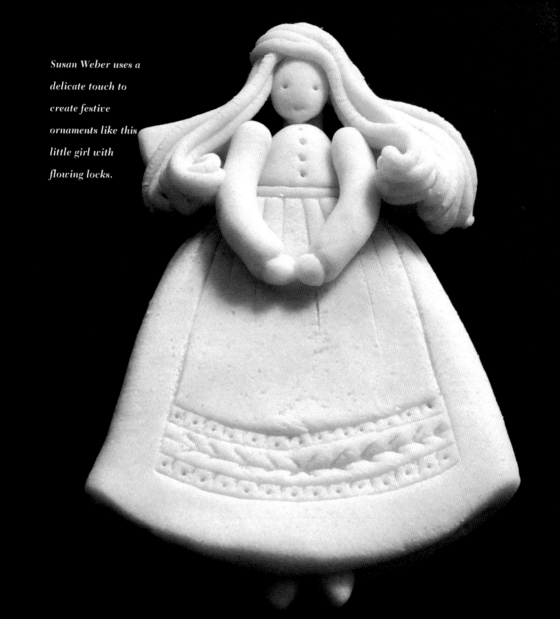

Susan Weber uses a delicate touch to create festive ornaments like this little girl with flowing locks.

Bread Dough Ornaments

With a little patience and a full imagination, the staff of life can be transformed into the stuff of Christmas. Susan Topp Weber transformed a hobby into a business making bread dough ornaments. When her son and daughter were small, Susan began making ornaments out of bread dough at home. As her children grew, Susan took her ornaments to craft shows, and then eventually expanded to a shop on Palace Avenue—Susan's Christmas Shop. Although it is filled with ornaments from around the world, the shop focuses on regional decorations. Susan still works at the same kitchen table and uses the same old gas range to create her well-known little Pueblo children and tiny Pueblo pots. ✮

Bread Dough Ornaments

Preheat the oven to 225° F.

Mix 1 part salt to 4 parts flour, adding just enough water to form a stiff dough. Knead the dough on a floured board until it is smooth and pliable. Roll out the dough on the floured board to the desired thickness (⅛ to ¼ inch) and, using a sharp paring knife, cut it into the form of your choice. (If you don't want to form your ornaments freehand, roll out the dough, then cut it with cookie cutters.) Use the knife to trim any ragged edges. To form flowing locks of hair, force a small ball of dough through a garlic press. Set the ornaments on a cookie sheet and bake for several hours. Turn off the oven and allow the ornaments to rest there overnight until they are "dog biscuit dry." When dry, the ornaments can be painted with acrylics. ✮

Celebrations

The *piñata* celebration is most closely associated with Christmas and, by extension, with the birthday of a child. Mexico invented the custom of the *piñata* as we know it today. Traditional *piñatas* were, and still are, made by covering a low-fired earthenware pot, or *olla*, with pieces of colored tissue paper. The *piñata* is then stuffed with sweets or little toys and hung by a rope. The most traditional shape is the star, no doubt for the star over the manger. Blindfolded children take turns at striking at the *piñata* with a stick until it has ruptured and the contents spill out and other children rush to gather the strewn goodies.

While Americans to the east spend hours picking out the right Christmas tree, Americans to the southwest can spend an equal amount of time choosing the right *piñata*. ✶

Friend Adam strikes the decisive blow, while Amanda and Thais survey the loot. Left: Thais clutches her share.

To make your own *piñata*, blow up a large balloon. Knot the end of the balloon and tie string to the knot (you will later hang *piñata* to dry). Make papier-mâché by adding flour to water to make a lumpy paste. Cut newspaper, magazine paper, and plain white paper into 2-inch strips. (White paper should be the last layer—it is easier to decorate than colored paper). Dip a strip of paper into papier-mâché paste. Remove the excess paste. Place the strip along the balloon and continue until you've covered the balloon with three complete layers. (A round *piñata* is easiest, but you can create other shapes by adding paper cones or molded paper towels, making sure to attach cardboard "struts" to the largest shapes to keep them from falling off.) Hang to dry.

When dry, cut a hole 4-inches in diameter, leaving one side uncut as a flap to be closed later. Decorate with paint or tissue-paper fringe—cut tissue into 2-inch strips and fringe one side with scissors; attach with glue thinned with water. (Begin at the base and work upward; careful—tissue colors will run.) Let paint or glue dry; fill with goodies; tape the opening shut; cover with more fringe; hang about five feet overhead and let children take their turns with the stick—under close supervision. ✶

Greetings!

Santa Fe greeting cards are touched by the same spirit of handmade, simple charm that characterizes so many of the local customs. Not content with store-bought greetings, Santa Feans have a long tradition of finding ways of personalizing each card. The established art colony of the 1920s and '30s probably had a great deal to do with the habit of making each card an individual creation—charming color woodcuts, ink drawings, etchings, and engravings. This spirit of individuality continues in the cards made from recycled Christmas cards, which have been carefully cut with special scalloped pinking shears and tied with a bit of ribbon.

Subject matter for Santa Fe greetings is picked with an eye for the regional, making *farolitos* and chile *ristras* among the most popular of local motifs. Everyone can make his or her own cards and wrapping paper with special stamps and colored inks. Cactus and stars, *farolitos* on an adobe wall, the symbol of the Santa Fe Railroad, a Santa Fe Santa wearing a Pendleton coat and a cowboy hat, adobe churches and a cheery "Feliz Navidad" are all appropriate symbols of a greeting from Santa Fe at Christmastime.

Lynette Wagner at Guadalupe's #1 A-OK Rubber Stamps and Crosses shop, up the stairs on San Francisco Street, offers so many stamps that choosing is never easy. She displays examples of what can be made at home, each card a little different, humorous, and heartfelt. ✱

Rubber Stamp Cards

For rubber stamp cards, choose a thick, glossy paper. Use a variety of stamps and several colors of ink pads to create borders (geometrics are best for these) and greetings. Then, using colored pens, fill in the designs. To finish the card, sprinkle embossing powder (which can be obtained where rubber stamps are sold) over it before it dries. Tap excess powder off the page and return it to the bottle. Hold the card carefully over a low flame—the powder will melt, forming a shiny raised image. ★

CHRISTMAS FOOD

Christmas Food

Feasting is a big part of the Christmas season in Santa Fe. Foods are hot and filling, spicy and subtle—the full range of a cuisine now popular across the country. The colors are those of Christmas, red and green, the same as the colors of the chile that is New Mexico's culinary mainstay.

Everyone cooks at Christmas. We look forward to a surprise treat of *empanadas* from a neighbor and a giant traditional pot of *posole* from our old friend Reynalda Ortiz y Pino Dinkel. Once school is over and the holiday begun, baking can begin in earnest. Downtown, Girl Scouts sell homemade *bizcochitos* on the plaza and steaming cups of hot chocolate are ladled up for those who brave the cold nights to attend Los Pastores. Christmas Day is a hurried breakfast of muffins before hours of opening presents. Then it's off to the Indian dances, maybe to Tesuque or San Ildefonso Pueblo, returning home with a huge appetite for a big elk stew or a New Mexican cassoulet, which has been simmering all day. ✳

Traditional empanadas from Anne Maryol, co-owner of Tia Sophia's restaurant, share a bowl with some red chile jelly, opposite. Josie Gallegos, of Josie's Casa de Comida, shows us some of what makes her Santa Fe's favorite cook, near left. This page, neatly tied tamales ready for steaming.

Josie assembles the Christmas burritos, right. On the stove at her Casa de Comida are the basic elements for numerous New Mexican dishes ready for the daily rush of happy chile addicts.

Christmas Burritos

Christmas burritos, or Christmas tree burritos, are actually served year round. Their primary purpose is to give those who have trouble deciding between red and green chile the opportunity to have both—any burrito can be a Christmas burrito if topped with both red and green chile sauces. The recipes given here are consolidations of some local favorites.

Pinto beans are also a mainstay of New Mexican cooking. Many New Mexican homes have an eternal pot of beans simmering on the back burner. Traditionalists claim that only a Taos Pueblo or Picuris Pueblo bean pot made of micaceous clay should be used for the preparation of pinto beans, but for the rest of us, long, slow cooking in a large, heavy kettle should do it.

3 cups pinto beans
2 garlic cloves
1 cup diced salt pork
Salt to taste
Bacon fat or vegetable oil
12 flour tortillas
Red Chile Sauce (recipe follows)
Green Chile Sauce (recipe follows)

Grated cheese (Longhorn, Jack, or Cheddar or a mixture of all three)

Wash the beans and soak them for at least 12 hours. Drain. In a large kettle, combine the beans and garlic and fill with enough water to cover the beans by 1 inch. Bring to a boil. Reduce the heat and simmer, covered, adding water as needed. After about 1 hour, add the salt pork and continue cooking for another 2 to 5 hours, until the beans are soft but not mushy. Remove the cover and cook until the liquid is reduced but not dry. Add salt to taste only when the beans are done.

To make the burrito filling, mash the beans or fry them in bacon fat or vegetable oil.

To assemble, heat tortillas on an ungreased griddle over medium-low heat. Wrap them in a tea towel to stay warm while you work. Spread ½ cup of hot bean mixture down the center of a tortilla. Roll the burritos, and place 2 burritos on a heatproof plate for each serving. Cover with Red Chile Sauce along one side, and Green Chile Sauce along the other. Top generously with grated cheese and heat under a broiler until the cheese is melted. Serve immediately.

Makes 12 burritos

Red Chile Sauce

This classic recipe is widely known and generally requires good-quality chile powder to produce a good-quality sauce.

1 garlic clove, minced
3 tablespoons olive or vegetable oil (old-timers prefer lard)
2 tablespoons flour
½ cup good-quality red chile powder
2 cups water
Salt to taste
Cumin and oregano to taste (optional)

In a medium-size skillet, sauté the garlic in the oil until softened. Add the flour and cook, stirring until the flour turns light brown. Add the red chile powder and cook for about 1 minute to release the flavor, taking care not to burn the powder. Add the water and the remaining spices. Stir and bring to a boil to achieve a sauce of medium consistency. This sauce can be chilled and stored for a few weeks for use in any number of dishes.

Makes 2 cups

Green Chile Sauce

One of the great harbingers of the coming winter in Santa Fe is the odor of roasting green chiles at the Farmers' Market and in the parking lots of the grocery stores. Purchased in gunny sack quantities, the roasted chiles are taken home, peeled, stemmed, and frozen for use throughout the year.

This simple recipe also depends greatly on the quality of the chiles, so try to obtain fresh or fresh frozen green chile. To roast your own chiles, first split, stem, and seed the chiles, and place them skin-side up under the broiler. After the skins have blistered, place the peppers in a pan covered with a cloth to allow them to steam; this will help to loosen the skins for peeling. When the peppers have cooled, remove the skins and chop. Always wear rubber gloves when working with chiles and be careful not to rub your eyes accidentally.

1 cup diced roasted green chile
1 small onion, diced
1 garlic clove, minced
Salt to taste
3 tablespoons olive or vegetable oil
3 tablespoons flour
2 cups water

Barely cover the bottom of a saucepan with water. Simmer the chile, onion, and garlic for 20 minutes. Add salt to taste and set aside. In a skillet, combine the oil and the flour and cook over medium heat until the mixture turns light brown. Add the chile mixture and the water and bring to a boil, stirring to achieve a sauce of medium consistency. Remove from the heat and let cool before refrigerating.

Makes 3 cups

Empanadas

These little pies are hearty morsels whose flavors range from sweet to salty. The meaty recipe given here should be used as a side dish or an appetizer.

2 tablespoons olive or vegetable oil
1 3-pound chicken, boiled, skinned, deboned, and chopped
1 large green bell pepper, seeded and chopped
1 large red bell pepper, seeded and chopped
1 large yellow bell pepper, seeded and chopped
1 large onion, peeled and chopped
1 cup peeled and chopped roasted green chile

2 teaspoons cumin
1 tablespoon chopped fresh cilantro
2 large tomatoes, chopped
8 ounces Monterey Jack or Cheddar cheese, shredded
4 frozen and thawed puff pastry sheets (approximately 12 x 8 inches)
1 large egg, beaten

Preheat the oven to 375° F. Cover the bottom of a large skillet with the oil and sauté the chicken, peppers, onion, chile, cumin, and cilantro until the peppers are soft. Transfer to a mixing bowl and let cool. Stir the tomatoes and cheese into the chicken mixture. Cut the puff pastry sheets into 4 ½-inch circles and brush one of each with beaten egg. Place ¼ cup of the chicken mixture in the center of each pastry and fold over to form a half-moon shape. Pinch the curved edge with a fork to seal. Brush the top of the pastry with the egg and place on a cookie sheet. Bake for 40 minutes or until golden brown.

Makes 12

New Mexican Cassoulet (*Cacerola*)

4 cups pinto beans
1 cup white wine
4 tomatoes, seeded and chopped
3 medium onions, diced
1 bay leaf
2 tablespoons chopped fresh cilantro
2 garlic cloves, minced
1 cup diced roasted medium green chile
2 pounds pork shoulder or butt (deboned)
Salt and pepper to taste
½ cup olive oil
1 pound chorizo
1 cup bread crumbs
¼ cup butter

Soak the beans overnight. Preheat the oven to 225° F. Drain the beans and place in an earthenware casserole. Add the wine, tomatoes, onions, bay leaf, cilantro, garlic, chile, and enough water to cover. Cover the casserole tightly and bake for 6 hours, adding water as necessary. Meanwhile, cut the pork into 1-inch cubes and season with salt and pepper. In a skillet, sauté the pork in the olive oil until browned. Remove the bean casserole from the oven and carefully stir in the meat. In the skillet, brown the chorizo, then stir into the casserole. Bake at 250° F for 1½ hours. Just before removing from the oven, sauté the bread crumbs in the butter in a small skillet; sprinkle over the casserole and continue to bake until the crumbs are well browned. Serve hot.

Serves 10 to 12

Bizcochitos

The state cookie can be found in every New Mexican home at Christmastime. It is both a delicate and a simple sweet.

1 cup (2 sticks) unsalted butter
1½ cups sugar
3½ cups flour
1 teaspoon baking powder
1 tablespoon anise seed
3 large eggs
½ teaspoon vanilla extract
1 teaspoon lemon zest

In a mixing bowl, cream together the butter and sugar until smooth. In a separate bowl, sift together the flour and baking powder and add the

SANTA FE CHRISTMAS

anise. Gradually add the dry ingredients to the butter-sugar mixture and combine well. Add the eggs, vanilla, and lemon zest and mix until you have a smooth dough. Cover the dough with plastic wrap and chill for 2 hours in the refrigerator.

Preheat the oven to 375° F. Roll out the dough on a lightly floured board to ¼-inch thickness. Cut into holiday shapes and place on a lightly buttered baking sheet. Bake about 10 minutes or until lightly brown.

Makes 2 dozen cookies

Chimayo Punch

This recipe is a play on the well-loved Chimayo cocktail, always made with tequila, and is wonderful for a Christmas gathering.

¼ cup water
½ cup sugar
2 cups fresh apple cider
½ cup fresh lime juice
½ cup tequila (*anejo*, or aged, is preferred)
½ cup Triple Sec
½ cup club soda
2 bottles champagne

1 tart apple, peeled, cored, and thinly sliced
2 fresh limes, thinly sliced

In a small saucepan, combine the water and sugar. Bring to a boil, reduce the heat, and simmer for 5 minutes. Let the syrup cool. In a large punch bowl, mix the syrup, cider, and lime juice. Add the tequila, Triple Sec, and club soda and keep cold with an ice ring. Just before serving, add the champagne and garnish with the apple and lime slices.

Serves 16 to 20

Cranberry Margaritas

A colorful twist on a favorite drink.

1½ ounces tequila
½ ounce Triple Sec
1 ounce cranberry juice
Juice of 1 lime
Lime slice for garnish

Combine all ingredients in a pitcher. Stir well and pour into a tall glass over ice. Garnish with a slice of lime.

Makes 1 serving

Yule Guide

Artesanos Imports
222 Galisteo Street
Santa Fe, NM 87501
(505) 983-5563
A national supplier of red chile wreaths and ristras, specializing in Mexican folk arts.

The Chile Shop
109 East Water Street
Santa Fe, NM 87501
(505) 983-6080
Salsa, gift boxes full of chile products, wreaths, and ristras. All the red and green of Santa Fe's chile can be found here.

Christmas at the Palace
Palace of the Governors
On the Plaza
P.O. Box 2087
Santa Fe, NM 87504
(505) 827-6463
Close to Christmas, an evening at the oldest public building in the United States is a night of music, entertainment, and, for the children, a visit with a very special Santa.

Christmas in Madrid
State Highway 14
The Turquoise Trail
Madrid, NM
And annual open house in a little semighost of a town that goes all out with displays from the town's heyday. Usually held during the first week of December.

Davis Mather Folk Art Gallery
141 Lincoln Avenue
Santa Fe, NM 87501
(505) 983-1660, 988-1218
Folk art from Hispanic New Mexico and Mexico. Each year, a special stock of Christmas snakes puts in an appearance.

Farolito and Luminaria Displays
Historic Santa Fe Foundation
545 Canyon Road
Santa Fe, NM 87501
(505) 983-2567
An organization that sponsors the annual displays on Canyon Road and Acequia Madre Street.

Guadalupe's #1 A-OK Rubber Stamps and Crosses
102 West San Francisco Street, Suite 5
Santa Fe, NM 87501
(505) 982-9862
A source of Santa Fe-style rubber stamps for all your needs, including making your own Christmas Cards.

Indian Dances in the Pueblos
Cochiti Pueblo (505) 465-2244
Jemez Pueblo (505) 834-7359
Nambe Pueblo (505) 455-2036
Picuris Pueblo (505) 587-2957
Pojoaque Pueblo (505) 455-2278
San Felipe Pueblo (505) 867-3381
San Ildefonso Pueblo (505) 455-3549
San Juan Pueblo (505) 852-4400
Santa Ana Pueblo (505) 867-3301
Santa Clara Pueblo (505) 753-7326
Santo Domingo Pueblo (505) 465-2214
Taos Pueblo (505) 758-9593
Tesuque Pueblo (505) 983-2667
Part of both the winter solstice and Christmas, dances are held throughout the season in all of the pueblos. These are not scheduled performances but sacred events which require respectful attendance. Check with newspapers, talk to locals, and call the pueblos to gather information regarding dances such as Matachines, Buffalo, Guadalupe Feast Day, Turtle, Deer, Comanche, Dawn, and Corn.

Jackalope Pottery
2820 Cerrillos Road
Santa Fe, NM 87501
(505) 471-8539
Crazy for Christmas, Jackalope provides everything from Christmas trees to chile lights as well as plenty of ornaments from around the world.

Josie's Casa de Comida
225 East Marcy Street
Santa Fe, NM 87501
(505) 983-5311
Just for lunch. During the week, this is a favorite spot for all of those who love red and green chile, especially in a Christmas burrito. Don't forget dessert.

Museum Shops

Museum of New Mexico Foundation
Main office, 116 Lincoln Avenue
Santa Fe, NM 87501
    Palace of the Governors (505) 982-3016
    Fine Arts Shop (505) 982-1131
    Folk Art Shop (505) 982-5186
    Indian Arts Shop (505) 982-5057
*Each of these museum shops, which support the various institu-
tion listed above, has a wonderful selection of cards, ornaments,
and gifts that are appropriate for the museum they serve and for
the Southwestern region.*

Los Pastores

Museum of International Folk Art
P.O. Box 2087
Santa Fe, NM 87504
(505) 827-6340
*An annual performance of this ancient folk play takes place at
the museum in mid-December.*

Paul's Restaurant of Santa Fe

72 West Marcy Street
Santa Fe, NM 87501
(505) 982-8738
*A number of recipes featured in the book find their home at
Paul's, a restaurant that does great things with regional flavors.*

Las Posadas on the Plaza

Museum of New Mexico
P.O. Box 2087
Santa Fe, NM 87504
(505) 827-6451
*A community-wide gathering for a performance of the folk play.
It takes place on the Plaza, one evening close to Christmas Eve.*

El Rancho de las Golindrinas

Route 14, Box 214
Santa Fe, NM 87505
(505) 471-2261
*A Spanish colonial-living history museum in La Cienega near
Santa Fe, which sponsors a traditional celebration of Christmas,
"Vamos Todos a Belen," usually the first week of December.*

Salvation Army

525 West Alameda Avenue
Santa Fe, NM 87501
(505) 988-8054
*Starting with a Thanksgiving dinner for the needy and the
homeless, this group seeks volunteers to help with its efforts to
bring Christmas cheer to the less fortunate. Opportunities to dis-
tribute gifts, sing carols, and donate toys.*

Santa Fe Chamber of Commerce

510 North Guadalupe
Santa Fe, NM 87501
(505) 988-3279
A good place to receive information about Christmas events.

Señor Murphy, Candymaker

P.O. Box 2505
Santa Fe, NM 87504
(505) 988-4311
*Gift candy with a distinct Santa Fe taste—including candies
with pinyon and chile.*

The Shop

208 West San Francisco Street
Santa Fe, NM 87501
(505) 983-4823
(800) 525-5764
*Loads of lights and hundreds of regional ornaments are avail-
able all year at this shop devoted to Christmas.*

Susan's Christmas Shop

115 East Palace Avenue
Santa Fe, NM 87501
(505) 983-2127
*The home of Susan Topp Weber's bread dough ornaments and a
great source for other regional ornaments.*

The Wheelwright Museum

704 Camino Lejo
Santa Fe, NM 87501
(505) 982-4636
*With a focus on traditional Native American art, this museum's
trading post has wonderful ornaments and often sponsors special auctions and events at Christmas.*

Index

References that are bold are to photographs